THAMES-SIDE KENT
THROUGH TIME
Anthony Lane

AMBERLEY

The author gained his first experience of the Thames shoreline from the motor ship *Royal Sovereign* in the late 1950s. Built in 1948, and seen here inward bound off Northfleet, the ship ran regular summer excursions from Tower pier to Southend and Margate until the service closed in 1966. Also featured in this picture are the Tilbury cargo jetty, at upper left, and the Swedish Lloyd Gothenburg ferries *Britannia* and *Suecia* exchanging places further downstream at the Tilbury landing stage, which is now the Cruise Terminal. (Aerobliques)

'Gravesend has a marvellous pageant of the ships of the world. It has something like a sea-front, a far better place of the kind than some seaside towns ... Every craft that sails the seven seas passes by, liners and tramps, tankers and barges, tugs and cargo boats, wherries and yachts. Here the whole world of trade, commerce and adventure seems to find a focus.'
Mee, Arthur, *Kent – The Gateway of England and its Great Possessions*. 1961.

First published 2011

Amberley Publishing Plc
The Hill
Stroud, Gloucestershire GL5 4EP

www.amberley-books.com

Copyright © Anthony Lane, 2011

The right of Anthony Lane to be identified as the
Author of this work has been asserted in accordance
with the Copyrights, Designs and Patents Act 1988.

ISBN 978 1 4456 0598 2

British Library Cataloguing in Publication Data.
A catalogue record for this book is available from
the British Library.

Typeset in 9.5pt on 12pt Celeste.
Typesetting by Amberley Publishing.
Printed in the UK.

Introduction

In the late 1950s, when in my teens and already a shipping enthusiast, I joined an excursion from Margate to the Pool of London aboard the *Royal Sovereign*, one of the General Steam Navigation Company's fast, modern motor ships that in summer travelled daily to Southend and the Kent resorts. It was my first contact with the varied features of the Thames riverside but from it was born an interest which has continued to the present day. I later travelled along the Thames aboard many different vessels and experienced the river in all weathers. During this period there occurred a total decline in sea training facilities and the disappearance of nearly all the industry on the Kent side.

Commencing at the Nore, this book follows the course of a ship inward bound, presenting a nostalgic study of the southern bank of the River Thames as far as the county of Kent extends, the mouth of the River Darenth, also known as Dartford Creek. Countless vessels of all sizes have travelled along these 31 miles of water over the centuries, some to one of the many wharves which lined the river and the majority to the earlier vast expanse of the London Docks.

In spite of a massive expansion of population the Kent riverside still has remote places, large areas of salt marsh, not quite as desolate as Dickens describes in *Great Expectations*, but still very sparsely populated. The northern part of the Hoo Peninsula still comprises large areas of marshland, for Allhallows, although anticipating growth in late Victorian times, never developed in the way of Southend opposite. At Cliffe, water-filled quarries formed by clay extraction have isolated the village from the river. In contrast, above Gravesend there has been, and still is, major development through Northfleet to Greenhithe and Dartford with Bluewater shopping centre and Ebbsfleet station catering for a multitude of shoppers and high-speed rail travellers, developments which ignore the Thames completely. Hence the Dartford Bridge and tunnels remain heavily congested and the river largely empty of traffic. Meanwhile, the once-busy Gravesend–Tilbury ferry has suffered from competition with the major crossings, struggling along subsidised and subordinated to a passenger only role.

In contrast, the relatively unpopulated banks of Long Reach above Greenhithe proved ideal for the mooring of isolation hulks to accommodate smallpox victims. Additionally, numerous wooden-walled training ships were moored at Greenhithe, Thurrock and Gravesend, to which were sent children who begged and stole, those who were poor, and those whose parents could afford to pay for a young man's training, either as seamen or officers. Over a period of 130 years a huge number of delinquent boys and career-minded cadets were trained aboard the *Arethusa, Cornwall, Exmouth, Shaftesbury, Triton, Warspite,* and *Worcester* to satisfy the needs of the nation's massive merchant and Royal navies.

Owing to the importance of London as a port over so many years, Gravesend has a long history of supporting the needs of shipping destined for the metropolis. Commencing with Henry VIII, and particularly after the incursion of the Dutch in 1667, the town was fortified in parallel with Tilbury to prevent an enemy from approaching the capital. Later, as the size and influence of London grew, pilotage, ship towage and customs and health examination vessels were all established at Gravesend by the early nineteenth century and nowadays, having lost ownership of the docks, the Port of London Authority is based there, in London River House.

Gravesend also provided entertainment for Londoners, achieving resort status in the early nineteenth century, when Jeremiah Rosher's creation, Rosherville Gardens, was regarded as a big attraction which even warranted its own landing pier. Furthermore, bathing machines were imported from Margate for the Clifton baths, which later adopted a striking oriental design. After 1815, paddle steamers brought many thousands from town by the 'Long Ferry' but the arrival of the railway had a detrimental effect, allowing the populace to travel further afield and as a consequence, sadly, Rosherville Gardens scarcely survived into the twentieth century, being gradually assimilated by Henley's cable works.

The southern Thames-side towns of Gravesend and Northfleet were subject to much industrial development during the late eighteenth and nineteenth centuries. Cement became the major activity after James Parker introduced his process to Northfleet in 1796 and vast amounts of the local chalk were quarried to feed the industry that equally developed at Greenhithe. Most of the cement firms were eventually united under the name of Associated Portland Cement Manufacturers (Blue Circle) and the last factory, operated by Lafarge Group from 2001, was not demolished until 2010. Papermaking also became important, the major players being Imperial Paper Mills at Gravesend, Bowaters at Northfleet and Empire Paper Mills at Greenhithe. Sadly, those and most of the other industrial wharves along these reaches have now closed, to be replaced partly by business parks and riverside apartments. Tower and Robin's wharves at Northfleet are, however, still thriving.

Finally, it is appropriate in this nostalgic review of the Kent riverside through time to include some of the often colourful characters who have worked on the river and faced the changes of ownership of their firms and reduction in numbers of crew employed. They have been the closest witnesses over the last three decades, a period when much of the character of the region has changed. Nowadays, Thames-side Kent, away from the solitude of the marshes, presents a mixture of affluent riverside apartments and derelict industrial sites. There is also a great contrast between the peace of the river and the adjacent complex road systems carrying enormous volumes of traffic. However, in places the rich history of the region is still discernible.

On a fine evening in October 1996, the inward bound Dutch product tanker *Anna Theresa* passes a vessel of the same company waiting for a pilot at the Warp, seaward of Southend. Further to the rear is the Red Sand fort. The Cypriot-registered, 2,000-ton *Anna Theresa* is bound for Jurgens jetty, Purfleet with a cargo of crude palm oil and glycerine. (A. L.)

The Nore lightship was anchored close to the above position for more than two centuries. The first of its kind, it was originally placed there as a private venture in 1732. Later taken over by Trinity House, its light guided mariners entering the Thames and Medway until it was replaced by a Maunsell anti-aircraft fort, manned by the Army, in 1943.

These Maunsell forts were arranged in the same way as the equivalent land battery. They were built at Red Lion wharf at Northfleet, the site of a cement works, and three were placed at the Nore Sand, Red Sand and Shivering Sands. Their relatively late introduction in 1943 meant they saw relatively little action, except to fire at V-1s, which they did with some trepidation. (A. L.)

The Nore fort was unfortunately hit in fog by the Norwegian vessel *Baalbek* in March 1953, causing two of the towers to fall, an event which resulted in the deaths of four of the ten civilian engineers aboard. As the fort lay close to the shipping channel, the remaining five towers and associated debris were removed, some resting to this day in Higham Bight near Cliffe Fort. The pictures on these pages are of the identical Red Sand fort. (A. L.)

Facing a freshening westerly wind, the motor vessel *Fisker* heads inward along Sea Reach in late 1997. Uncaring about the weather, the ship's cat Gerba sleeps peacefully in its basket in the wheelhouse. The wide expanse of water here off the oil refineries of the Essex shore disguises the narrow channel which ships must follow, for the Blyth Sands extend a long way out from the Kent side. (A. L.)

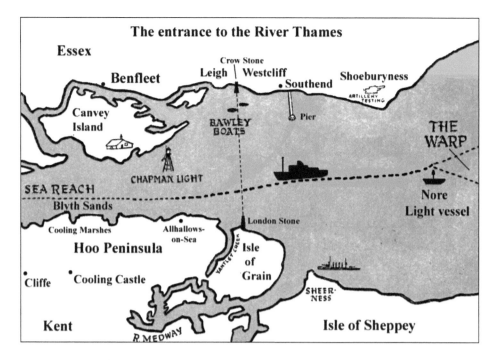

Most of Sea Reach is shown here, with an indication of the salient features on both banks. Vessels loading explosives earlier anchored near the Chapman light, an activity now transferred to Alpha Jetty, Cliffe. The imaginary line between the London Stone and the Crow Stone once formed the official limit of the Thames Conservancy. (After A. G. Thompson)

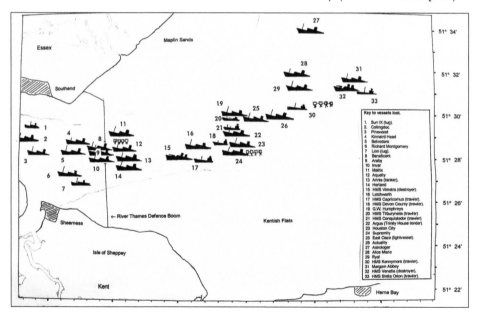

Magnetic mines laid by the Germans early in the Second World War took a heavy toll on shipping entering and leaving the Thames. Most of the vessels indicated here were sunk by that cause, one exception being the East Oaze lightship, which was lost with all her crew due to air attack. (A. L.)

Cooling Castle was built between 1381 and 1385 by John de Cobham to defend the River Thames. In 1554 the castle was besieged by Thomas Wyatt and suffered damage from cannon fire. Lord Cobham offered brief resistance and then surrendered. It has a double bailey; the western one, surrounded by stone walls with a tower at each corner, appears in this engraving of May 1784. (S. Hooper)

The castle was afterwards abandoned and is still mostly in ruins, but the impressive gatehouse remains in good condition. In more recent years a private house was constructed inside the grounds. Nowadays, it is nearly two miles from the river. The adjacent picturesque barn caters for weddings and other social occasions. (A. L.)

Cliffe Fort is a more recent contribution to the defence of the Thames. As a result of a Royal Commission of 1859, work began in 1861 and the building was completed by 1870. Originally equipped with 12.5-inch and 11-inch muzzle-loaded guns, it fell into disuse in the twentieth century except for war service and is now derelict. The nearby Shornmead Fort and Coalhouse Fort on the Essex side of the river were built in the same period. (A. L.)

A novel type of weapon was installed at Cliffe Fort in 1895 in the form of a wire-guided torpedo invented by Louis Brennan. Launched from this rail, the missile was guided by a twin-wire arrangement controlled by an engineer who took directions from an officer in a look-out. There were originally two such rails at Cliffe. (A. L.)

B.F.GRIBBLE

In August 1901, the *Gravesend Reporter* recorded 'A Submarine Missile Incident.' The Goole ketch *W. S. Flower* had left Tilbury dock laden en route for her home port when she was struck and holed off Cliffe by a Brennan torpedo fired from the fort. Although armed, the torpedo lacked a detonator and fortunately there was no explosion. The ketch sank in about twelve minutes, sufficient time for her owner, Captain Bartlet, his wife, Mr. Brunt, mate, and Mr. Sheppard, cook, to safely abandon ship into their boat. (B. F. Gribble, *Black & White* Magazine)

Above: The first navigation light encountered on the Kent shore is Shornmead lighthouse, established by Trinity House at the much later date of 1913 to mark the bend of Higham Bight where Gravesend Reach meets the Lower Hope. Unwatched, and automatic in operation, it was recorded in 1961 as showing a double flash every ten seconds at a height of forty feet. (A. L.)

Left: The Port of London Authority took over the ownership and maintenance of the Thames lights in 1993. By 2001 the tower above had become unstable due to erosion, and it was replaced early in 2004 by this pile lighthouse. The low-lying marshland behind is evident in both photographs. (A. L.)

One craft that has changed little for more than a century and a half is the Thames spritsail barge. Vast numbers of them carried a great variety of cargoes from the London docks to all the ports on the south-east coast before the final few found active retirement as pleasure craft. The history of racing continues and *May* is shown above running with all sails set in Sea Reach in the 1998 Thames barge match. (A. L.)

On a day with far less wind, *May* and *Edme* wait in Lower Hope prior to the start of the 1996 match. (A. L.)

Bargemen do not change greatly either, except nowadays more are carried than simply the master and mate of the hard commercial days. Brian 'Bowie' Weaver is shown at the helm of *Repertor* at the entrance to Sea Reach around 2009. Brian has frequently crewed with skipper David Pollock over the last twenty years. (A. L)

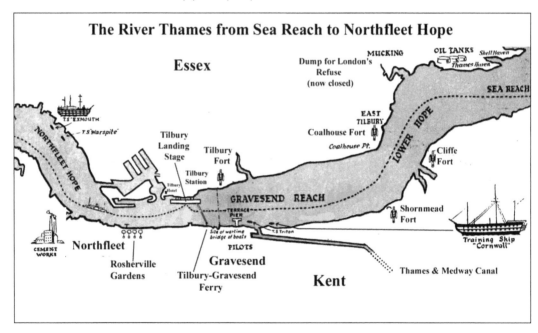

Between the Lower Hope and St Clement's Reach, the Thames provides much of interest. Evidence remains of the Tudor fortifications at Gravesend and Tilbury and the former town has earlier connections with smugglers. Many of the service craft which served London's shipping became based at Gravesend and much industry developed along the banks here. (After A. G. Thompson)

Approaching Gravesend, the first commercial site encountered is J. Clubb's marine aggregates operation. They have a quarter-mile-long jetty at Denton with a conveyor belt capable of allowing dredgers to discharge some 2,500 tons per hour. Ashore lies a maze of gantries, conveyors and silos covering 11 acres, similar to Brett's site at Cliffe. (A. L.)

A little further upstream lies Denton wharf. Originally a commercial wharf with a fine selection of cranes, as seen here in the late '90s, the structure at that time was found to be unsafe, leading to its being dismantled and the cranes sold or scrapped. It was purchased by the Port of London Authority (PLA) and totally rebuilt in 2000–2003 as a base for their service craft, with an extra pontoon for Svitzer's tugs. (A. L.)

The Ship and Lobster public house lies close to Denton wharf and was as a consequence owned briefly by the PLA. Early records suggest that it was built in 1813 as The Ship, a name by which it was known in *Great Expectations*. Closely connected with smugglers, it apparently gained its present name around 1832. The building illustrated is thought to date from 1890 but despite a rather dark past, it is nowadays popular with local ship repairers. (Photochrom Co.– B. A.)

In the nineteenth century the Seaman's Hospital Society had premises at Denton for the isolation of those with infectious diseases. Precautions are being made against cholera in this graphic illustration of 1892. Incoming ships were routinely inspected by staff of the Port of London Sanitary Authority based at Gravesend, who used the hulk *Hygeia* moored offshore as an initial examination base before transfer to the nearby isolation hospital. (*Illustrated London News*)

The Thames and Medway Canal was opened in 1824, but was not a commercial success and a railway line was later laid along the greater part of its route. This house, which lay near the canal at Gravesend, had an upturned boat as the roof. The owner rented out pleasure boats on the canal to visitors. Apparently referred to by Charles Dickens, it was demolished in 1942. Sadly, the canal is now very much overgrown. (Thornton Bros., New Brompton)

The canal basin at Gravesend has become a marina offering moorings to house boats and yachts of various sizes. The marina apartments of Venture Court which overlook the basin resemble a much more modern ship. Nearby, the Gordon promenade has for many years offered an interesting view of the river and the possibility of a pleasant stroll. (A. L.)

Left: Gravesend has had a long association with the training of boys for service at sea. The Sea School was established in 1918 to train deck and catering boys for the merchant navy, occupying part of what had once been the Commercial Hotel. Later, that building was replaced by these new and larger premises. (Shipping Wonders of the World)

Below: A move to a new location on Chalk marshes was made in 1967 and the buildings in Commercial Place mostly demolished in 1975. Re-named the National Sea Training Trust, the purpose-built college replaced both the old Gravesend Sea School and the TS *Vindicatrix* at Sharpness. However, such was the decline of the British merchant fleet that in 2003 the new site became a Metropolitan Police College.

HM Customs have always had a strong presence on the Thames. A supplement to the *Saturday Magazine* of April 1834 states that: '12,000 revenue officers are always on duty on the river!' This was equal to the number of watermen. Gravesend was the initial place for examination and this cutter, *Enterprise*, was one of a fleet of craft employed by the rummage crews in the mid-1930s. (Shipping Wonders of the World)

The customs vessel *Searcher* arrives off Gravesend in the late 1990s. Much larger in size, she was designed for the examination of craft in coastal waters as well as the Thames Estuary. Customs activities have now mostly moved away from Gravesend. (A. L.)

This atmospheric sketch of Gravesend riverside made from Royal Terrace Pier in 1906 typically includes the ubiquitous Thames barge. Bawley Bay and the St Andrew's Mission are rather hidden but the lead works are visible at near left, as is the Town Pier in the distance. (Hugh Thomson)

Reminiscent of earlier years, this picture was taken directly off the St Andrew's Mission House at the time of the 1997 barge match. The buildings are, from right, London River House, the new Port of London headquarters; the older, red-brick Thames Navigation Service building; Royal Terrace Pier; and Alexandra House. (A. L.)

Military activities increased at Gravesend and Tilbury in times of conflict. At the end of the 1770s a strategic ferry, known as the 'communication' was installed between the two forts to ensure the rapid transit of large numbers of troops. In this engraving, Lt-Gen. Pierson's force is using the 'communication' to make a mock attack on Tilbury Fort in 1780. In the First World War a pontoon bridge was constructed to link the two places. (F. West – 1785)

Completed in 1795, the New Tavern Fort at Gravesend had sixteen smooth-bore, cast iron guns with a range of 2,900 yards installed, strengthening the defence of the river considerably. Over the years the guns were replaced and the fort improved, but it never saw action, save to fire a salute. Nowadays, a range of preserved weapons is displayed there, including this 6-inch MK VII gun. (A. L.)

Gravesend N. Kent

Above: Gravesend grew in importance as a resort in the nineteenth century. This engraving of 1832 shows the busy waterfront and High Street just before the Town Pier was built. The town had a population of about 10,000 at that time. (J. Fussell, J. Henshall)

Left: Sailing craft carried travellers both down and across the Thames before the arrival of steam, the crowded and competitive 'tilt' boats having awnings to protect passengers from the weather. This sailing boat is approaching the West Street Pier, which later became the berth for the vehicle ferries and is the point of departure of the Tilbury ferry today. (S. Hildesheimer & Co.)

The Clifton baths offered immersion in warm, tepid and cold sea water; warm cost three shillings and cold one shilling in 1824. Bathing machines had first been brought in from Margate in 1796, one appearing in this engraving of 1828. By 1834 a lavish, oriental-style covered swimming pool had been opened and the Clifton Hotel built alongside. (G. Shepherd, H. Adlard)

Records show that in 1821 some 27,291 persons landed or embarked at Gravesend from London. Ten years later that figure had increased to 240,000, mostly due to the popular paddle steamers apparent in this engraving, which also shows the improved Clifton baths. The steamer *Vesper* and her companion in the foreground were owned by the Star Steam Packet Company. (W. H. Bartlett, H. Adlard)

Although Customs personnel were present at Gravesend much earlier, this Custom House was completed in 1816 on the site of the former Fountain Tavern. Although for a long time the London Custom House gave the required clearance, the closure of the upriver docks led to this impressive building becoming the headquarters again in 1990 for a further five years. It is now a museum. (A. L.)

Situated adjacent to the Royal Terrace Pier, dating from 1844, Alexandra House is of much more recent construction, being built in about 1976 following the takeover of the London tugs by the Alexandra Towing Company. The car park nearby was previously an oil depot. (A. L.)

Right: Born in Virginia in 1595, the American Indian princess Pocohontas saved the life of Captain John Smith, leader of the British settlers at Jamestown. Baptised as a Christian in 1613 she married John Rolfe, another settler and bore him a son. They came to England in April 1616, and were entertained at Court. However, Pocohontas became ill, and died at Gravesend in March 1617 on her return voyage to America. In 1958 the people of Virginia presented this statue to the town. (A. L.)

Below: General Charles Gordon was associated with Gravesend for a much longer period, residing in the town between 1865 and 1871. Most famous for his participation in the siege of Khartoum, he was responsible for the construction and modernisation of most of the lower Thames defences, including the New Tavern Fort. Besides his military achievements, he contributed greatly to the care and education of the poor of the town. (A. L.)

25

This nostalgic view of Gravesend riverside captures the atmosphere of the 1930s. The sailing barge *Scone* lies in 'Bawley Bay,' while the Gravesend–Tilbury passenger ferry *Catherine* and a Watkins tug enliven the mid-ground and an Orient liner at the Tilbury landing stage completes the picture. (Shipping Wonders of the World)

Notable among the different vessels permanently moored off Gravesend was the reformatory training ship *Cornwall*, which started her career at Purfleet but moved to Denton in 1928. Originally the 74-gun, third rate ship *Wellesley*, the ship was built in 1815 at Bombay Dockyard. Lent by the Navy as a training ship for the School Ship Society in 1859, her career ended when she was set afire and sunk during an air attack in September 1940. Some of her timbers were used in the post-war reconstruction of the Law Courts in London.

Adjacent to the New Tavern Fort, the Gordon promenade has been a popular place for strollers for many years, offering excellent views of passing shipping. (Thornton Bros., New Brompton)

Terrace Pier was built in 1844 on Doric iron columns. It gained the title 'Royal' after Princess Alexandra of Denmark landed there in 1863 on her way to marry the Prince of Wales. The pier became a base for the pilots, who were supervised by a 'Ruler'. Ownership eventually passed to William Watkins, Gamecock and Elliott's tugs, who shared the offices and pontoon in the post-war years. Eventually the accommodation was removed and nowadays the pontoon is used by PLA service craft. (A. L.)

Royal Terrace Pier pontoon in 1997, with the new Harbour Master's patrol launch *Benfleet* alongside. She was at least the third to bear the name. The pilot launch *Patrol* also worked from the pier, as well as the PLA hydrographic vessels. Public access to this pier ceased in the 1990s after the pier master retired. (A. L.)

In parallel with the Medway and Leigh-on-Sea downriver, Gravesend was well-known for its fleet of shrimping bawleys in the nineteenth and twentieth centuries. A few remained until as late as 1965. These vessels had moorings in what became known as 'Bawley' bay, next to the St Andrew's Mission in Royal Pier Road. (Bell's Photo Co., Leigh-on-Sea – B. A.)

A recent view of the St Andrews Waterside Mission. It was 'designed to furnish the means of religious consolation and instruction to sailors, emigrants and fishermen.' In 1872, mothers' meetings took place there, together with sewing classes, a clothing club, Bible classes and night schools for boys and girls, all under the superintendence of the clergy. It is now an art centre. (A. L.)

As the landing facilities at Gravesend were becoming inadequate, a wooden pier was built in about 1831, but this was burnt by protesting boatmen. In contrast, the iron Town Pier dating from 1834 has lasted to the present day. After the passenger ferries moved to the West Street Pier it fell into decay, but was restored at the time of the millennium. (A. L.)

The London, Chatham & Dover Railway (LCDR) pier was built close to West Street station in 1886. Boat trains brought passengers to board steamers such as the Dutch *Batavier II* for passage to Rotterdam in the 1920s, and later to MV *Royal Daffodil* for post-war excursions to France. White Horse ferries were built on this pier in the 1990s, but it is now disused. (A. L.)

William H. Muller's 1,500-ton steamer *Batavier II* dated from 1921, and except for the war years, provided a regular passenger service between London and Rotterdam which continued until April 1958. The ship was broken up at Utrecht in 1960.

The dining saloon aboard *Batavier II* appears very comfortable given the small size of the ship. Accommodation was provided for ninety-three First Class and fifty-three Second Class passengers. (Batavier Line)

28148 Gravesend. The Yacht Club.

Clifton Marine Parade afforded an excellent view of the river and provided much of interest for the discerning visitor. This view shows the New Thames Yacht Club at left, which was previously the Clifton Hotel. Further along are the bathing station of 1797 and the Clifton baths, rebuilt in an oriental style. Most of these buildings were replaced by the Imperial Paper Mills and, more recently, apartments, but part of the area lies derelict today. (Photocrom Co. – B.A.)

The view up river today from the West Street Tilbury ferry landing stage shows how apartments have replaced the commercial sites below the LCDR Pier. Commercial Wharf, Town Wharf and Marriot's Wharf, which occupied the stretch between the two piers, are no longer recognisable. (A.L.)

Although this picture shows the new Iranian short sea trader *Persia* inward bound off Tilbury in 1958, the main interest lies in the view of the Imperial Paper Mills opposite. Wood pulp stocks and the mill buildings extend for a considerable distance, as far as the White House, which is still in existence. Reeds eventually took over the firm but closed the mill around 1985. Imperial Jetty and the long-demolished power station are visible at extreme right. (Robert Gore)

Imperial Paper Mills were founded in 1912 by Alfred Harmsworth, later Lord Northfleet. Large quantities of wood pulp from Canada were unloaded at their jetty. Coal for the mill's power station is also being unloaded from Stephenson Clarke's collier *Totland* in this view, which faces in the opposite direction to the one above. The site is now mostly occupied by the Imperial Business Park. (E. T. W. Dennis & Sons)

Half a century ago, wood pulp was brought to Bowater's Northfleet paper mill nearby by vessels such as the 4,000-ton *Elizabeth Bowater*, seen here in Sea Reach in July 1963. An effort was made in those days to give a distinctive design to each company's ships. (Robert Gore)

The Kent papermaking industry being much reduced, nowadays large quantities of paper and other forest products are delivered to Tilbury dock by advanced ro-ro vessels such as the 20,000-ton Swedish flagged *Ostrand*, *Obbola* and *Ortviken*. Such vessels are designed to maximise cargo carrying capacity and minimise the cost of operation. (A. L.)

Captured passing Gravesend outward bound in the late 1950s, the 9,400-ton Norwegian freighter *Roland* was built in Germany in 1956. In this atmospheric picture, a passenger ferry has just left the Tilbury landing stage and a car ferry waits alongside the West Street Pier. The *Roland* became the Greek *Kirin* in 1965 and was wrecked in 1976. (A. L.)

Nowadays, roll on-roll off (ro-ro) ferries form a major part of the Thames traffic. Cobelfret offer a regular service to Zeebrugge and Rotterdam from their Purfleet wharf. The 24,000-ton *Victorine* is seen inward bound in Gravesend Reach. Dart Line offered a competitive service from Dartford International Freight Terminal (DIFT), but this company was taken over by Cobelfret some five years ago and all services are now operated from Purfleet. (A. L.)

The earlier elegance in design of ships is also evident in the German-built *Indian Splendour* of 1957, bound up-river past Gravesend, probably for Tilbury dock. The vessel was owned by India S.S, giving lengthy service until broken up at Bombay in 1979. Ships of another Indian company, Scindia S.N., also sailed regularly to London. (A. L.)

Just under forty years later and more representative of today's ships in size, the *Republica di Roma* passes Tilbury inbound with a pilot launch alongside. This 42,000-ton ship built in 1992 is a container ship with ro-ro capability. She is also bound for Tilbury dock. (A. L.)

Also inward bound is New Zealand Shipping Company's 10,000-ton cargo liner *Otaki*. Here representing a type of vessel owned by many famous British lines, she was a product of the famous John Brown's yard at Clydebank in 1953 and was not broken up until 1984. During her service with NZSC she carried the Victoria Cross awarded posthumously to the master of the previous *Otaki*, which was sunk in March 1917 after an epic fight with the raider *Moewe*. (New Zealand Line)

The changes to a ship's appearance brought about by containerisation are apparent in this view of the *P&O Nedlloyd Remuera* passing Gravesend in 2003. The ship has a now rather modest gross tonnage of some 44,000 tons, and with no cargo-handling gear is dependent on the shore-side cranes of the Northfleet Hope container terminal. P&O withdrew from the ownership of container vessels shortly after this date, but still operate ro-ro ships such as the *Norqueen* to Tilbury dock. (A. L.)

A classical British freighter of the late 1950s, the *Cairnforth* moves slowly upriver while the pilots are exchanged off Gravesend. Established in 1876, the Cairn Line traded across the Atlantic to Canada. One of the smaller British companies, it was absorbed into a larger combine, in this case Furness Withy, who ceased to trade in 2005. After having six further names, the ship was wrecked off Libreville, Gabon in 1979. (A. L.)

Bulk cargo carriers developed from the 1950s onwards, tankers, colliers and ore carriers eventually reaching enormous proportions. Typical of the smaller-sized dry bulk vessels of 12,000 tons (20,000 deadweight) or so is the Japanese-built *Aikaterini L*, seen outward bound off Northfleet in 1997 after discharging a cargo of sugar at Tate & Lyle's Silvertown refinery. Many different vessels were chartered for this service. (A. L.)

Ocean liners were always of most interest to ship enthusiasts at Gravesend. Most of the larger P&O and Orient liners used Tilbury dock and would land and pick up their passengers from the Landing Stage after its opening in 1930. This pre-war view shows the *Comorin*, one of the P&O intermediate liners, in the earlier colours of black hull with white line and ochre superstructure, approaching the old entrance to the dock. (H. Y. Scott, Gravesend)

Orient Line's 20,000-ton *Orontes* of 1929 is swung by tugs in Gravesend Reach in this later view. Best-looking of a series of similar ships, she ran to Australia for most of her working life, her last voyage being in November 1961. She was broken up at Valencia the following year. (H. Y. Scott, Gravesend)

Also voyaging to Australia, the P&O 'Strath' liners were slightly larger. The *Strathnaver* was built in 1931 at Barrow, and with her sister *Strathaird* was the first to be painted white. Both originally had three funnels, but the two dummies were removed after the last war to increase deck space, and in 1954 they became one-class ships with berths for 1,200 passengers. *Strathnaver* was broken up in 1962 at Hong Kong. (H. Y. Scott, Gravesend)

Illustrating the modern design in cruise ships, which replaced the liners, the luxurious *Silver Whisper* of 2001 is operated by Silversea Cruises of Fort Lauderdale. She is shown moored alongside the Tilbury Cruise Terminal. Most cabins have balconies on these latest ships. (A. L.)

Above: A trans-Atlantic liner, later turned to cruising, and a stranger to the Thames, was the Swedish-America vessel *Gripsholm*. This 23,000-ton ship, built in 1957, ran for many years between Gothenburg and New York. She is seen here sailing outward past Gravesend around 1975. Visible also are the Town Pier, some moored 'LASH' barges, St Andrews Mission, the lead mill where the new PLA offices would be built and Royal Terrace Pier.

Right: Another Swedish company sailing from Tilbury landing stage was Swedish Lloyd, whose ships *Britannia, Suecia, Saga* (shown here) and *Patricia* provided a regular ferry service to Gothenburg until 1976. This illustration is taken from the company's timetable for the summer of 1950, when there were up to four sailings weekly in each direction. Passengers would mostly arrive by boat train from St Pancras Station.

In terms of ship towage, W. H. J. Alexander's 'Sun' tugs were regarded as the smartest on the Thames in their day. *Sun XI*, *Sun X*, *Sun XVI* and *Sun XVII* are shown at their Gravesend moorings in the 1950s with two of Watkins' tugs on the buoys astern. Other interesting features are a vehicle ferry crossing at left and the P&O liner *Carthage* or *Corfu* alongside Tilbury landing stage.

In this closer view, *Sun V* escorts an outward bound Yugoslav freighter in Gravesend Reach. Note the double-decker buses exported as deck cargo. *Sun V* was built at Hull in 1915 and eventually sold to a Neapolitan firm in 1966. She was scrapped at Naples in 1979.

Gamecock Steam Towing Company's blue-funnelled *Crested Cock* is about to leave Royal Terrace Pier, probably to berth a ship in conjunction with the tug from which the photograph was taken. The 177-ton *Crested Cock* was built in 1935 and served on the Thames until scrapped at Antwerp in 1970.

A much later design of tug passes the modern Gravesend waterfront, the wheelhouse concealing the older London, Chatham & Dover Railway pier. *Lady Cecilia* was one of five sisters built around 1991 for Howard Smith for service on the Humber. Now named *Svitzer Cecilia*, in line with the colours she bears, this tug is vastly more powerful and manoeuvrable than her predecessor above. (A. L.)

The Voith-propelled tractor tug *Sun Anglia* dates from 1985. Seen here in 1996 in Howard Smith colours with Tilbury dock as a background, her name combines earlier W. H. J. Alexander and William Watkins' names. She now berths ships on the Thames under the name of *Svitzer Anglia*. (A. L.)

Ken Sutherland, master, left, and mate Tony Tree at the helm, reflect upon the latter's recent experiences at handling a single-screw tug, having always been used to Voith-propelled vessels. Ken has since retired to a riverside apartment and his son David has become a skipper. Tony Tree is also now a master. (A. L.)

Screw-propelled ship-berthing tugs have now left the Thames. This picture shows the retrieval of the towline by capstan aboard the *Sun Essex* in November 1997. *Sun Essex* and her sister *Sun Kent* were both built in 1977. In the final days they had five crew and those shown here are, from right, David Watson, Tony Watson, Sean Strong and Duncan Savage. (A. L.)

Another Voith tug is *Sun Surrey*, built in 1992 and seen here with master Les Hills at the helm. Les was also convenor for the Transport and General Workers' Union for Howard Smith. He later retired and is now a councillor for Gravesham. *Sun Surrey* has also left the Thames. (A. L.)

A comparable group of Howard Smith's tugs moored to the Gravesend buoys in July 2001. They are, from left, *Sun Surrey*, *Ganges*, *Sun Thames*, *Cobham* and *Shorne*, the last two recently purchased from Dover Harbour Board. (A. L.)

The Thames tugs not only berth ships, they are also equipped to fight fires. When the Kimberley Clark warehouse at Northfleet caught fire in July 2004, the conflagration reached major proportions. Adsteam's *Sun Sussex* and *Redcliffe* helped to fight the fire, the former attending for sixteen hours and also supplying water to ten fire engines. (Shawn Scutts, engineer of *Sun Sussex*)

In this conventional ship-handling operation in April 2008, Svitzer's *Lady Cecilia* has made fast to the centre lead at the bow of the 32,000-ton forest products carrier *Star Istind*. *Adsteam Redbridge* holds the stern and the two will shortly swing the ship to line up with the entrance lock to Tilbury dock. (A. L.)

In almost the last view of a working tug, Cory Environmental's *Regain* hauls a group of empty barges up Gravesend reach from the Mucking dump to Charlton or beyond. As the Crossness refuse-fuelled power station is now in operation, this river traffic ceased around March 2011 and the Mucking disposal site is to be closed. (A. L.)

Above: Moving on to pilotage, John Godden trained with Alfred Holt's Blue Funnel Line and afterwards moved in 1954 to the General Steam Navigation's pleasure steamers, sailing often on the *Royal Daffodil* from the LCDR pier at Gravesend. In 1965 he became a Trinity House pilot on the Thames, transferring to the PLA in 1988. He was also for a time editor of *The Pilot* journal.

Left: Thames pilot Roger Harris leaves the inward bound 50,000-ton Norwegian car carrier *Nosac Star* at Gravesend in April 1995. Deckhand David Newton waits aboard the cutter *River Thames* to guide him safely aboard. (A. L.)

Above: The busy approaches to the River Thames consist of relatively narrow channels between sandbanks. Pilots can sometimes encounter language difficulties, as in this case between pilot Richard Taylor and the Russian captain of the *Levant Weser*, inward bound from Salerno in 1993. Yorkshireman Richard Taylor, a Younger Brother of Trinity House, later retired to France. (A. L.)

Right: David Newton stands by the helm of the Gravesend pilot cutter *River Thames* in April 1995. He worked with coxswain Ian Wight for some years on that cutter but later transferred to the Woolwich ferry to join his son Scott. (A. L.)

Many cutters have served the pilots over the years, including this pre-war *River Thames*. Gravesend has been the place where, traditionally, the exchange of the sea and the river pilots took place. Nowadays sea pilots are licensed to take vessels as far upriver as Crayford Ness, which means there are fewer river pilots than formerly, but those remaining now work from Putney as far out as Sea Reach No. 1 buoy. (Shipping Wonders of the World)

This newer, post-war *River Thames*, seen in 1995, similarly landed and shipped the pilots from the upper deck, a distinct advantage with high sided vessels. She had a sister, the *Pilot*, but both eventually proved too slow and were replaced by newer and faster launches, firstly the *Patrol*, then the *Benfleet*, and now the *Southwark*. (A. L.)

Deckhand Roger Wilson stands ready to tie up the *Patrol* to the pontoon at Royal Terrace Pier. The *Patrol* was originally built for Trinity House as a cutter at Harwich, but was sold to the PLA around 1988–90 for service at Gravesend. She has recently reached the end of her service. (A. L.)

Marcus Wright, then a newly licensed PLA pilot, leaves the Dutch vessel *Ideaal* of Sneek at Gravesend in June 1996. The ship was carrying 1,080 tons of rice, which was taken firstly to Seabright wharf for fumigation, and then to the Tilda Rice terminal. Marcus, who comes from Cheltenham, has now become one of the fifteen duty port controllers. (A. L.)

All commercial craft entering the Thames must report by radio to Port Control, London. Their movements are monitored by the Vessel Traffic Services Team (VTS) from the building in Royal Pier Road, Gravesend. Here Radio Officer Jim Cartlidge, at rear, discusses vessel movements with Duty Port Controller Roger Mantle in the mid-1990s. (A. L.)

This recent picture emphasises the progress achieved in fifteen years. Philip Dalton, nearest, and Ian Cosgrave are on VTS duty in the same area of the PLA building as above. Increased radar coverage, CCTV of important wharves and reaches, much improved displays and more comprehensive processing of ships' and agent's details make this a truly impressive system compared with earlier years. Automatic identification of vessels has also recently added to the safe working of the river. (Port of London Authority)

Right: Steve Wright served aboard the coastal tankers of Bowker & King between 1970 and 1977. He then joined the PLA Middle District Thames patrol crews in June 1977, becoming a coxswain at the age of twenty-six. Having been established as launch master in 1984, he served at Gravesend until July 2007, completing thirty years in total with the PLA. He is now a master aboard the high speed Thames Clippers. (A. L.)

Below: The PLA launch *Gunfleet* moored at Royal Terrace Pier. Steve Wright and his crew, Frank Wilder and Gerry Roberts, made regular patrols of the river from Sea Reach to Barking Reach with this launch and the *Benfleet*, checking for any contravention of the river regulations and generally assuring the river was safe for navigation and working wharves well maintained. Until the RNLI lifeboats arrived, they also acted in a search and rescue role. (A. L.)

Three other crews also manned the patrol launches. Launch Master Barry Smith is at the helm of the *Gunfleet* at the mouth of the Thames in April 1995. Barry started as a fireman on the Gravesend tugs and joined the PLA in the early 1980s. He also left the PLA in 2007 and, having been a strong swimmer for many years, became an instructor. (A. L.)

The late Gerry Donald Roberts enjoyed a very varied life on the river. He began as a boat boy rowing lightermen about the roads and later became a pierman at Greenwich. He worked for a number of years with Union Lighterage before joining the Lower District Thames patrol launches as deckhand. Seen here taking his turn as cook, he was a great character, always capable of witty, humorous and sometimes incisive comment. (A. L.)

Charles Crawley began supplying water to ships on the Thames in 1880 from Wapping. In 1940 the firm moved to Gravesend's Town Wharf, and after the war operated four X-craft which had served at the Dardanelles during the First World War. These armoured barges were named *Aqua*, *Aquator*, *Aquarium* and *Aquaduct*. One of them is shown here, with the steamer *Archgrove* in the background. (C. Crawley)

As more wharves were directly connected to a mains water supply, Crawleys gradually changed to oil bunkering, a move that gained in emphasis when Esso, BP and Charrington, Gardner and Lockett ceased to provide a service. The 594-ton *Aqueduct*, seen passing Gravesend in 2002, was originally Charrington's *Charcrest*, which was built in Dartford Creek. (A. L.)

Three of Crawleys' bunkering barges lie moored to the run-down Town Pier in 1996. *Perfecto* retained her name from her Shell Mex and BP days, *Doverian* was purchased for bunkering at Dover and *Fulford* was originally Charrington's *Charmo*. All these were sold before Thames Shipping Services took over Crawley's assets at the start of the new millennium. (A. L.)

Thames Shipping Services commenced with the barges *Aquatic*, *Aqueduct*, *Bruce Stone*, *K. Toulson*, *Marpol* and *Tommy*. The last-named, seen here off the promenade at Gravesend in 2001, was Bowker and King's *Batsman* until 1987. The company nowadays operates as Thames Fuels, supplying oil with the *Conveyor* and *Torduct*, while the *K. Toulson* is used for storage. (A. L.)

Passengers can still travel on the lower Thames on a regular basis in summer aboard John Potter's *Princess Pocahontas*. Owning the only Thames pleasure steamer with a sea-going passenger certificate, he offers regular trips in summer for up to 207 passengers up-river as far as Greenwich and Chelsea and seaward to Southend. (A. L.)

The Paddle Steamer Preservation Society vessels *Waverley* and *Balmoral* offer a short programme of trips on the Thames and around the estuary each year from Tilbury. In contrast to the usual views of idyllic Scottish lochs, PS *Waverley* is seen here passing the now-demolished cement works at Bevans Wharf, Northfleet in 1996. (A. L.)

Small and inconspicuous compared to the *Waverley*, the *Higham* was a tender built for the Alexandra Towing Company to carry crews from Royal Terrace Pier to tugs moored on the buoys. Peter Boyd, her coxswain, also a model maker, maintained the *Higham* to the highest standard. Not wishing to be parted on retirement, he made a metre-long model of her, which he now sails on Bluewater Lake. (A. L.)

White Horse Ferries ran the Gravesend–Tilbury passenger ferry from March 1991 until 2002, firstly with their locally built catamaran *Great Expectations* and later with the small trimaran *Martin Chuzzlewit*, seen here approaching the specially adapted West Street Pier. She proved too unstable for the frequently rough conditions and strong tides of Gravesend Reach and was sold to work upriver in more sheltered waters. (A. L.)

Some kind of cross-river ferry has existed in the Gravesend area since Roman times. The service varied considerably over the years but once Henry VIII had built Tilbury Fort, military needs encouraged a more reliable operation. After the railway companies took over the ferry in the 1850s, more than a century of consistent running was achieved. This typical view shows a ferry alongside the Town Pier around 1900. (Wrench Series)

The *Edith* was built as a passenger and vehicle ferry in 1911 for the London, Tilbury & Southend Railway, but passed the following year to the Midland Railway. Later carrying passengers only from Town Pier, her last sailing was on 28 February 1961. This postcard is one of a commemorative series by artist Ian Boyd.

The Town Pier entrance as it appeared in the late 1920s. In 1923, due to amalgamations, the LMS took over the service and it remained under their ownership until the nationalisation of the railways in January 1948. One other feature of this picture is the gentlemen's 'pissoir' at left, which appears well ventilated. (Thornton Bros., Gillingham – B. A.)

A diesel-propelled *Edith* replaced her predecessor in 1961. Able to carry up to 475 passengers, she and her sisters, *Catherine* and *Rose*, were the last of the railway ferries. In 1965, due to the scrapping of the old vehicle ferries *Mimie* and *Tessa*, the service was transferred to the West Street Pier. *Edith* became redundant after White Horse Ferries took over, but remains a houseboat on the Thames.

John Potter, left, owner of *Princess Pocohontas* since 1989, has had a long association with the river. He spent four years with Silvertown Services, three with *Flower* and *Everett*, then a time with Westminster Dredging, followed by seven years with Shell Mex and BP before going alone with the *Pocohontas*. John Barrett, mate, can claim sixty years on the Thames, including twenty years with each of Braithwaite & Dean and Humphrey & Grey. (A. L.)

Since the summer of 2002, John Potter has also operated the Tilbury–Gravesend ferry with the *Duchess M*, here seen approaching West Street pier. She was built in 1956 as the *Vesta* for the Porsmouth–Gosport ferry service. Her sale to Thames owners occurred in 1974 and she obtained her present name in 1978. A spell on the Tyne commenced in 1991 before her return in 1997 to Southend for five years of running sea trips and estuary crossings. (A. L.)

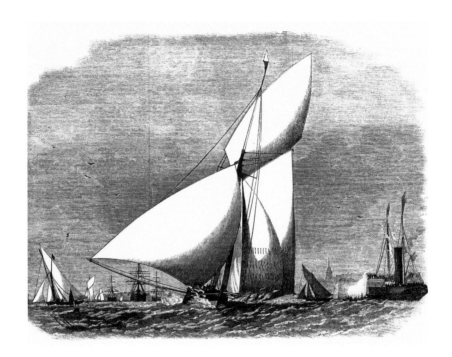

Yachting became a very popular sport in the lower Thames in Victorian times, with regular regattas and races to round the Nore lightship. Popular clubs included: the Royal Thames, New Thames, Junior Thames, Temple, Corinthian and the Nore. This engraving shows the *Fiona* winning a Royal Thames Yacht Club match at Gravesend in 1865. (*Illustrated London News*)

Modern barge 'races' involve much more effort and much less speed. At the time of the Gravesend Shrimpers' annual regatta, a series of crews row traditional 'dumb' barges down river from Greenwich over two days, with a stop at Erith. Held to support the Dreadnought seamen's hospital charity, the crews consist of freemen of the river supported by energetic volunteers. (A. L.)

The Gravesend illustrations end with two final scenes of passing shipping. In this first from the 1950s, Elder Dempster's *Sherbro* heads seawards for West Africa. She follows in the wake of a Swedish short sea trader heading for the continent, while a British collier is foremost. Such a procession of smaller ships following high water at the London Docks was typical of those years.

At certain states of the tide, the river at Gravesend is still busy. The inward bound 32,000-ton ro-ro vessel *Roxanne* passes the intermediate container ship *Joanna Borchard* in July 2002. In contrast, neither of these vessels has a berth beyond Tilbury. (A. L.)

Northfleet progressed from its rural origins to become a highly industrial area, led initially by chalk quarrying and lime kilns. Shipbuilding became important with the arrival of William Cleveley in the eighteenth century. This engraving of 1809 shows Thomas Pitcher's later shipyard at far left and St Botolph's church on the skyline at right. (S. Owen, W. Cooke)

This aerial view shows part of the Northfleet industrial area around 1970. Northfleet power station, at upper left, was opened in 1963 and closed in 1991. It was built on the Red Lion cement works site. A large area to the right is occupied by Henley's cable factory, later AEI, which first encroached upon and then almost completely occupied the original area of the attractive Rosherville Gardens.

Enjoying fine river views, the impressive residence of Crete Hall was owned in its early years by Jeremiah Rosher through his marriage to the daughter of Benjamin Burch. Rosher masterminded the construction of the 'new town' of Rosherville and the creation of the famous Rosherville Gardens in a disused chalk quarry nearby. Sadly, Crete Hall was demolished in 1937 when Henley's cable factory was enlarged. (R. Ackermann's Repository of Arts, 1826)

22001 Rosherville Gardens

Rosherville Gardens were opened in 1839 as a zoo and botanical garden. They became very popular with Londoners in mid-Victorian times, having a landing pier provided for steamers. Other attractions were later added, including an archery lawn, a maze, a Baronial Hall used for dances, a House of Marvels, Bijou Theatre, bear pit and lake. The tower by the entrance was built in 1864. (The Photochrom Company – B. A.)

The upper terrace of Rosherville Gardens reveals that quiet areas were available besides the popular attractions. Sadly, the lake was filled in around 1887 and the gardens closed in 1900. The next year they were refurbished and reopened during the summer months until 1910. After that, they became derelict until the area was developed by Henley's Telegraph Works between 1924 and 1938.

Three of Jeremiah Rosher's interesting buildings still remain in Landsdowne Square, but the Rosherville Hotel, which stood in the north-western corner of the square, was demolished in 1968 and only the steps remain of the once-popular pier. This is now a conservation area, although the riverside is severely littered. (A. L.)

Henley's cable factory was built in the grounds of Crete Hall, Northfleet in 1906 and was later enlarged as described below. The firm was eventually taken over by AEI but the site now lies largely derelict, their art-deco office building being almost the only one surviving intact. (A. L.)

Standing to the western side of Henley's site lies the Red Lion pub, identical in name to the cement works which stood opposite and where the Thames anti-aircraft forts were built. Records suggest a pub has stood near here since 1755, although the former building was closer to the river. The Red Lion now hosts numerous gigs, with musicians coming from a wide area. (A. L.)

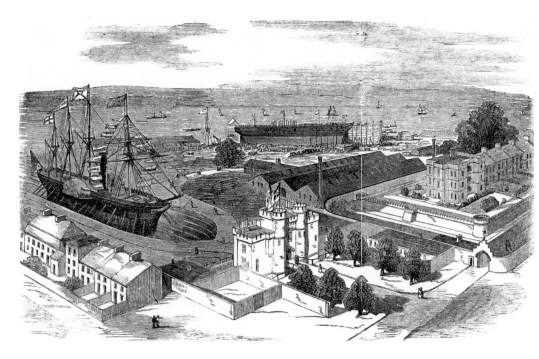

Thomas Pitcher's Northfleet shipbuilding yard was established in 1788. His sons, William and Henry, later extended the site to become one of the most important on the Thames. This engraving celebrates the launch of the 2,245-ton mail steamer *Orinoco* in May 1851. Also notable is Brunel's *Great Western* in the 500-foot-long dry dock. The dockyard, with its saw-pits, smithery and mould loft, occupied an area of about 14 acres. (*Illustrated London News*)

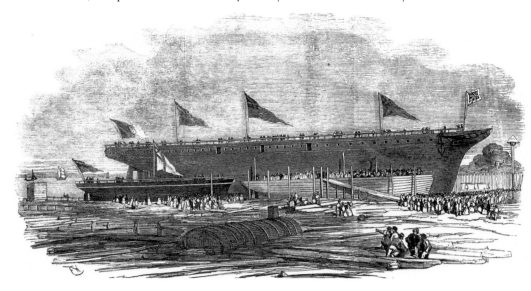

Two ships were launched in September 1854 from William Pitcher's yard. The smaller was HM Gunboat *Pelter*, the first of four to be built for the Navy, the others being *Pincher*, *Ranger* and *Snapper*. The larger was the Portuguese screw steamer *Dom Pedro Secondo*, built for a Brazilian company to run between Lisbon and Rio de Janeiro. Every last trace of this famous yard would eventually be covered by Bowater's paper mill. (*Illustrated London News*)

Little indication of the industrial future of Northfleet appears in this early nineteenth-century engraving of what appears to be the Creek. James Parker built lime kilns near the Creek in 1796 to manufacture his Roman cement, the beginning of a huge industry which spread right along the river, with nine different works between Swanscome and Gravesend alone by 1900. (Dugdales)

This later view of Northfleet Creek shows how the cement works had developed by the early years of the twentieth century. Robin's works here were later taken over by Knight, Bevan and Sturge, becoming part of Bevan's works. Today, Robin's wharf is operated by Foster Yeoman and handles bulk coal, coke and aggregates. (Mrs Rodway, The Post Office, Northfleet – B. A.)

ROSHERVILLE GARDENS, MAIN ENTRANCE.

Left: The tower at the main entrance to Rosherville Gardens in London Road was built in 1864. It had a clock with a musical chime playing characteristic tunes after the style of a French carillon. Having outlived the gardens it finally fell victim to the expansion of Henley's works, being demolished in 1939. (Thornton Bros., New Brompton)

Below: As the cement industry initiated by James Parker and William Apsdin grew, the number of manufacturers increased. The various firms eventually became combined into Associated Portland Cement Manfacturers, but Bevan's Wharf retained its original name from Knight, Bevan and Sturge. Three trademarks relating to Northfleet cement manufacturers are inset. This view shows the site in 1996, before ownership had passed to Lafarge. Everything except the office block at centre was demolished in 2010. (A. L.)

Right: Bowaters were the other major papermakers at Northfleet. Their office tower was built around 1957, at a time of expansion and union with the Scott Paper Company. Kimberley Clark Corporation acquired Bowater Scott in 1995 and their present tissue factory can be seen at the rear of this picture. Currently, this interesting building lies neglected and it is hoped it will avoid the same fate as the tower at Rosherville Gardens. (A. L.)

Below: Bevan's Wharf in 1997, with an appropriately-named ship alongside. Northfleet lower navigation light (now disused) is visible at far left and the upper light can just be seen on top of the office block. The latter remains important to river users. Cement is still imported to this wharf. (A. L.)

William Watkins' was one of the oldest Thames towage companies. Based at Gravesend, they were involved in coastal salvage and ship towage along the length of the Thames as far as the Pool of London. The steam tugs *Cervia* and *Badia* here assist a ship at the entrance to the Royal Docks in the 1950s. Ensuring the availability of tugs over more than 25 miles of river still presents problems. *Cervia* is now preserved at Ramsgate harbour.

This photograph of Tower Wharf, Northfleet was taken by the author from the *Royal Sovereign* at about the position shown in the frontispiece. She is passing the outbound Dutch coaster *Oranje*, typical of the 'schoots' of fifty years ago. (A. L.)

Howard Smith's tugs *Sun Surrey* and *Sun Thames* assist the departure of the bulk carrier *Golden Trader* from the outer berth of Tower Wharf in 2001. The current operators are Seacon Terminals Ltd. Cargoes handled include steel, non-ferrous metals and forest products. (A. L.)

Forest products are imported to this inner, covered berth at Tower Wharf. Seacon Terminals have a fleet of four 2,000-ton coasters in this trade, which currently accounts for 25 per cent of all cargo handled at Tower Wharf. The adjacent Robin's Wharf, which handles aggregates and other building products, can be seen, as well as the cement works beyond Northfleet Creek. (A. L.)

Tilbury docks lie only a short distance across the river from Northfleet and are now the only dock system remaining on the Thames. Close by in the river is the Northfleet Hope container terminal, seen here, with the large Tilbury grain terminal at left. Ships of the German Hamburg-Sud(amerikanische) D.G. are regular callers. The 69,000-ton *Monte Cervantes* dates from 2004 and is one of the largest ships to visit the terminal. (A. L.)

Broadness light, left, marks the change from Northfleet Hope to St Clement's Reach on the Kent side. There has been a light here since 1885 and this triangular steel trestle tower dates from 1981. Earlier lit by acetylene gas, since 2003 it has employed a diode array powered by solar and wind energy. The much larger tower at right carries high-tension electricity cables across the river beyond Broadness. (A. L.)

A cross-river link of high-voltage electricity lines was first constructed near Dagenham in the early 1930s. Those cables were carried on pylons 417 feet tall. They were replaced in about 1960 by the towers on Broadness (shown here) and West Thurrock marshes. The distance apart of 1,500 yards provides a minimum air draft of 250 feet for passing shipping. Not quite as intricate as the Eiffel Tower, but with a height of 623 feet, they are the tallest in Britain. (A. L.)

As the Thames has been a major artery for shipping, collisions were in the past a common occurrence, some minor and some, like the *Princess Alice*, tragic. Recorded here is the dramatic encounter between the Margate steamer *Duchess of Kent* and the *Ravensbourne* off Northfleet Point in July 1852, the former sinking in about nine minutes. Incredibly, all passengers were saved from the stricken vessel by the rapid action of the crews of the *Ravensbourne* and *Meteor*. (*Illustrated London News*)

Another collision victim was the Gravesend United 'Ring' tug *Britannia* of 1887. She sank in April 1909 off Tilbury Ness after colliding with the London County Council sludge steamer *Bazalgette*. Her captain, J. Curtis, and mate, Frank Box were the only survivors from a crew of seven but the *Britannia* was salved, repaired and continued in service well into the 1930s. (Yankee Studios – B. A.)

Passenger vessels were earlier in collision off Greenhithe in the evening darkness of December 1845. The steamer *Emerald*, on her way down river to Gravesend, was struck by the Hamburg packet *John Bull*, proceeding inward. Panic ensued on the *Emerald*, which fortunately remained afloat, and her drifting against a brig anchored nearby allowed all those aboard to escape to safety. (Illustrated London News)

This last casualty, the dredger *Arco Arun*, struck the Black Shelf on the Essex shore in October 1998. In a sinking condition, the vessel anchored west of Broadness Point, out of the shipping channel, but unfortunately capsized. She was not raised until 29 November and is seen on that date with Thurrock in the background. Older readers may remember the saga of the East German vessel *Magdeburg*, which sank in the same place in October 1964. (A. L.)

Greenhithe suggests a rural position by the water, which was partly true at the time this engraving was made, around 1840, but chalk has been quarried there from at least the fourteenth century. Its position close to Watling Street and the Thames made access easy and the consequential industrial development and urbanisation has drastically changed this view today. (Tombleson, Varrall)

The cement industry brought wealth to Greenhithe but also reduced its appeal, such that it became like Northfleet, which John Thorne described thus in his Kent guide: 'white dust clinging to the roofs and walls give many of the houses a ghostly grey appearance'. The scale of the cement silos is suggested by Donald Maxwell in his drawing 'The Giant Jars of Greenhithe' from the 1920s.

While much has changed at Greenhithe over the past two centuries, the site of Ingress Abbey, which dates from around the fourteenth century, has remained. Here also the tenant of the estate in Tudor times was allowed 'the liberty to dig and carry off chalk.' In 1649 the mansion house, manor, farm and lands, lime kiln, wharf, salt and fresh marshes passed to Captain Edward Brent of Southwark for £1,122. (S. Owen, W. B. Cooke – 1829)

As part of a plan for a large dockyard between Northfleet and Greenhithe, the earlier 'abbey' was summarily demolished in 1830, but the project was never realised. Alderman James Harmer commissioned a new abbey to be built using reclaimed stone from the old London Bridge to a design by architect Charles Moreing. More recently the site was acquired by the Thames Nautical Training College, whose ship the *Worcester* was moored offshore. (A. L.)

"Arethusa", Greenhithe.

A number of training ships graced the riverside at Greenhithe from Victorian times. The National Refuge for Destitute Children, later the Shaftesbury Homes, moored there both the ex-HMS *Chichester* (1866) and ex-HMS *Arethusa* (1874), the latter, shown above, remaining until 1932. (H. & L. Payn, the Bazaar, Greenhithe – B. A.)

Boys exercise on the deck of the *Arethusa* around 1900. Many children from poor backgrounds received an education and training in seamanship aboard the various ships at Greenhithe, Thurrock and Gravesend. (Marshall, Keene & Co.)

The Thames Marine Officer Training School was opened in 1862 using HMS *Worcester*, loaned by the Navy. A permanent mooring was found at Greenhithe in 1871, and a further ship, the 74-gun ex-*Frederick Wilhelm*, became the second *Worcester* in 1876. After the Second World War, a third *Worcester* was obtained. Shown above, she was previously the Metropolitan Asylums Board's *Exmouth*, earlier moored at Thurrock, built of iron and steel in 1905 as a training ship, rather than a conversion. (Bob Appleton)

In 1938 the Thames Nautical Training College, as it became known, acquired the famous tea clipper *Cutty Sark*, which was moored next to the *Worcester* until a permanent berth was prepared for her at Greenwich in 1954. In 1968 a new Merchant Navy College was built on land at Greenhithe and the *Worcester*, being redundant, was sold to be broken up in 1978.

The Wall Paper Works, Greenhithe.

A training ship also appears in this view of the Empire Paper Mills at Greenhithe from about 1906. Another important mill on the south bank of the Thames, it was later purchased by the Reed Paper Group along with Imperial Paper Mills at Gravesend. Eventually closed, it was recently demolished and the site is now derelict. (B. A.)

The Merchant Navy College at Greenhithe absorbed the Thames Nautical Training College in 1968. At first it was successful, but afterwards fewer boys sought a career at sea in Britain's rapidly declining merchant navy, leading to its closure around 1995. Sadly, this impressive institution was demolished to make way for the large building programme of riverside apartments. (A. L.)

Another Greenhithe institution was the shipping firm of F. T. Everard & Sons. Dating from about 1889, a hive of industry, their yard provided maintenance facilities for their sailing barges and steam and motor coasters until its closure almost a century later. This painting shows their sail loft. (Frank H. Mason)

This impression of Everard's blacksmith's shop also reveals the bows of two of their coasters hauled up on the slipways. (Frank H. Mason)

Everard's operated a large fleet of coastal tankers and dry cargo ships. All had black hulls initially but commencing in the 1950s, the larger motor ships were painted yellow, an unusual and stimulating choice for those days which was eventually extended to all of their dry cargo fleet including MV *Stability*, one of their later ships. Since the takeover by James Fisher, the colour has been discontinued. (B. Pawley, World Ship Society)

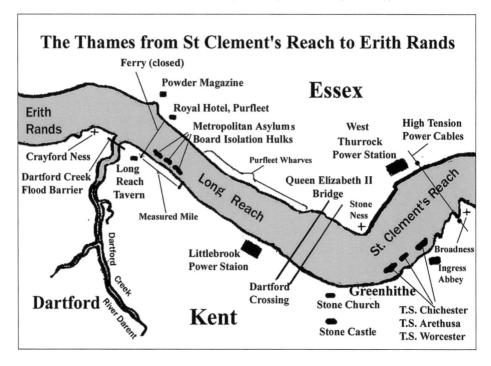

The reaches of the Thames leading to the boundary of Kent at Dartford creek. The positions of the important features are indicated. (A. L.)

High Street in Greenhithe still boasts some older buildings like the Pier Hotel, but modern developments encompass it on all sides. The Pier Hotel was formerly the Admiral Keppel Inn. The buildings here and in Pier Road are reminiscent of the time when numerous visitors landed at the elegant 350-foot pier between the mid-1840s and 1875, seeking the town's 'rural and sylvan scenes.' (A. L.)

The modern waterfront apartments at Greenhithe extend for a considerable distance, being constructed in part on the sports field of Ingress Abbey, as used by the *Worcester* cadets. A mosaic monument to the famous training establishment has been laid at the seaward end to the drive, which reveals the Abbey when viewed from the water. (A. L.)

85

A notable and historic building not too far from the river is Stone Castle. Originally built in about 1140, only a 40-foot-high tower of that period remains. Most of the house seen in this engraving dates from 1825. In the early 1900s, it was occupied by the managing director of a local cement works and remained with Blue Circle Cement management until 2000, when it became the Heritage Conference Centre. (Fussell, Mottram – 1829)

Nearer to the river, on a bluff at Stone, stands the parish church of St Mary the Virgin. Designed by an architect associated with Westminster Abbey, this beautiful building, earlier referred to as the 'Lantern of Kent', dates from the thirteenth century. (A. L.)

The view down river from the lower end of Long Reach in 1963. Visible in the distance are West Thurrock power station, demolished in about 1996, and the high-level cross-river power transmission lines. The vessel *Vega* of the Stockholms Red. A/B 'Svea' company is inward bound, passing roughly the present site of the Dartford crossings. (Robert Gore)

Although the first Dartford Tunnel dates from 1964, the Queen Elizabeth II Bridge was not commenced until August 1988. It was built by the Cleveland Bridge & Engineering Company to a design by German civil engineer Hellmut Homberg for £120 million. (Rod Chalmers)

The final sections of the cable stay bridge are placed in position. It was completed early in 1990. (Rod Chalmers)

A tranquil scene on the river in April 1997 as a yacht sails down stream. The elegant Queen Elizabeth II Bridge adds a note of grace to the highly industrialised area it adjoins. In the background stand the buildings of the Dartford International Freight Terminal, which is now disused. (A. L.)

There is nowadays a great contrast between the number of river users and those who cross it by road. Alone on the Thames, the coaster *Ariel* sails inwards in Long Reach, shortly to pass under the bridge, which carries around 70,000 vehicles a day. (A. L.)

A normal mid-morning scene at the Dartford Crossing tolls in the spring of 2011. Such congestion is a far cry from the peace of the Cliffe and Cooling marshes, where this journey began. (A. L.)

Two other examples of ships in Long Reach are included. In April 2000, the bulk carrier *Hermes II* heads upriver for Tate and Lyle's sugar refinery at Silvertown, just beyond the Woolwich Barrier. Ships of this type have regularly brought cargoes of around 20,000 tons of raw cane sugar to the Thames refinery. In recent years, however, the emphasis has changed to more locally grown beet as the source. (A. L.)

Sailing outwards from Crossness on the 9-hour round trip to the Barrow Deep, the sludge vessel *Thames* approaches Dartford Bridge. Noted for their regularity, the *Bexley*, *Hounslow* and *Thames* sailed together on almost every tide from Crossness and Beckton until Thames Water's operation closed on 31 December 1998. Richard Beet, master of MV *Thames*, remembers that the ship's record for sailings was 650 tides out of 704 in one year. (A. L.)

A/B Rod Chalmers at the helm of *Bexley* about a month before the service closed. The ships were steered manually as far as Southend and then went to automatic pilot, which guided them to the very accurately monitored sludge deposit ground off Clacton. After the ships were withdrawn, Rod moved to the collier *Sir Charles Parsons*, which supplies Kingsnorth Power Station on the Medway. (A. L.)

Just above the Queen Elizabeth II Bridge lies Littlebrook power station. Initially completed in 1939, it was later enlarged. The buildings of this first station are seen painted white at left, now devoted to office and other accommodation. At right stands the replacement station, completed in 1981, which is held in reserve in case of a sudden fall in supply. This building has the third highest chimney in England, standing at 705 feet. (A. L.)

Smallpox had become a scourge by 1881 and three ships were obtained by the Metropolitan Asylums Board (MAB) to isolate sufferers from the community. Two were moored at the upper end of Long Reach in 1883, and consisted of the *Atlas* of 1860, originally intended as a 91-gun man-o-war but never fitted out, and the *Endymion* of 1865, a frigate. *Atlas*, seen here at the upstream end, had 120 beds while *Endymion* became an administration vessel.

A third vessel, *Castalia*, here seen at the rear, was added in 1884. She was a double-hulled experimental vessel intended to relieve sea-sickness on the Dover–Calais ferry service, but proved unsuccessful. She was fitted out with ten wards to accommodate 154 female smallpox cases. The three ships remained on the moorings until 1903, when the Joyce Green Hospital was opened on land nearby after some 20,000 cases had been treated afloat. They were then broken up. (London County Council)

Nearby Long Reach Tavern was notorious for cock fighting and bare-knuckle prize fights. Its remoteness made these illegal pursuits possible, and should the law be seen approaching, a convenient escape lay in the ferry across to Purfleet. This point was also the position of the upper post marking the measured mile. Dartford Brewery Company and Style & Winch owned the tavern, which was flooded in 1953. Later a victim of fire, it was demolished. (Kent Libraries and Archives)

Nowadays, the sport of clay shooting takes place only a short distance inland from where the Long Reach Tavern once stood. Dartford Clay Shooting Club has an enthusiastic regular membership with social events, and also welcomes newcomers to try their hand at the sport. (A. L.)

Most of the Thames reaches above Gravesend now have flood defences. These are mostly raised walls or earth embankments, but at Dartford Creek (the River Darenth) a barrier has been built. Dating from 1981, it prevents tidal flood-water from reaching Dartford and Crayford. The building comprises two 160-ton gates balanced by water-filled counterweights in each of the towers, resulting in the need for very little power to lower and raise them. (A. L.)

Crayford Ness, at the top of Long Reach, is the point where the supervision of river navigation passes from Gravesend to Woolwich. It is also the inward limit for sea pilots. Visible in the picture are, from left, the Kent side of the Dartford Bridge, Littlebrook Power Station, the Dartford Creek flood barrier and finally the lattice tower and light marking Crayford Ness. Thus ends our journey along the Thames through time. (A. L.)

Acknowledgements

While this book is to some extent a personal record of changes to the lower reaches of the River Thames made in my lifetime, it owes a great deal to the encouragement and help of a large number of river users.

The first of those is the Port of London Authority, who originally, with the help of Mike Whitton and the late Mike Belsey, introduced me to a number of the pilots. Further, I owe my sincere thanks to Dot Knight of the Vessel Traffic Services Team, John Clandillon-Baker, Duty Port Controller and editor of *The Pilot* journal, and Steve Wright of the Thames Patrol launch. Finally, I record my sincere thanks to Steve's colleague the late Gerry Roberts, that living legend of the watermen, whose sharp wit and dry humour enlivened any Thames lower district patrol.

Equally helpful have been the shore management and crews of the tugs of Alexandra Towing Company, later Howard Smith, Adsteam and nowadays Svitzer. I express my gratitude to Steve Leach, John Reynolds, David Brown, Kevin Boyd (son of the famous Frank who shortened Southend Pier) and Steve Harris for their help with information and arranging visits aboard numerous tugs over the years.

Although only briefly mentioned in this work, I am deeply indebted to two other concerns that use or have used the river. Firstly, Timmy Keach and John Walker of Cory Environmental, almost the last of the lighterage firms, whose crews demonstrated to me their skill in collecting and manoeuvring London's refuse barges daily to Mucking, traffic that only this year ceased to pass Gravesend. Secondly, masters Roger Bremner, Dick Beet and Royston Potter, of the 'Royal Flush' of sludge vessels *Bexley*, *Thames* and *Hounslow* respectively, and their crews, who awarded me their 'Chain Puller's Diplomas' for discharging the cargo in the Barrow Deep, certificates I still treasure. Their daily journeys ceased at the end of 1998.

There are many books about the River Thames, but I have found A. G. Linney's *Peepshow of the Port of London* and *Lure and Lore of London's River* (circa 1930) very helpful for his description of the lower reaches, together with L. M. Bates' *The Londoner's River* (1949). The various works of A. G. Thompson for travellers on the river in the 1930s are also enlightening. These books describe a riverside that has all but disappeared.

Lastly, I am grateful particularly to Bob Appleton, earlier a resident of Gravesend, for local information and allowing me to reproduce a number of postcards from his large collection which carry the initials B. A. My photographs bear my initials.

About the Author

Anthony Lane trained as a scientist but has a life-long interest in ships and the sea, devoting time to the maritime history of the Kent coast in particular. He has published articles for local history and shipping journals and written several well-known works on local shipwrecks as well as a history of the port of Dover, *Front Line Harbour*. Anthony is married with two daughters.